COSTUME CAMEOS 1

by
Hazel Ulseth & Helen Shannon

TABLE OF CONTENTS

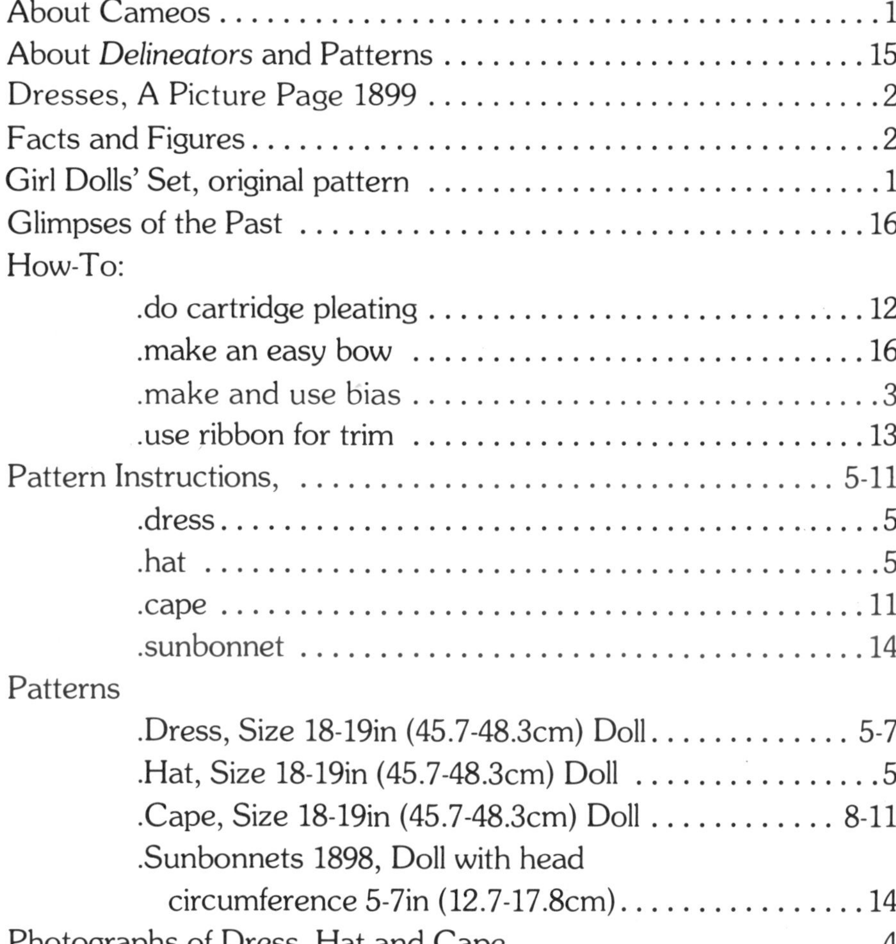

Published by

HOBBY HOUSE PRESS, INC.
Cumberland, Maryland

ISBN: 0-87588-204-8

ON COSTUME CAMEOS

We think costuming dolls is fun...a rewarding hobby and a pleasant offshoot of doll collecting. It does not matter what kind of dolls one collects — almost all need clothes since, unfortunately, not too many "original garments outlive the ravages of time, of dampness, of moths and silverfish, of the wear and tear of little owners not so kind to silken fabrics, furbelows and feathers."

So we offer replacement possibilities consistent with the period, the styles and fabrics of the times...our contribution to doll collecting. If we add a little pleasure and a little expertise to your hobby, that is our reward.

In this booklet you will find a few interesting facts relating to doll costuming, some pages of children's dress styles of 1899 taken from *Delineator* magazine, a page of variations on little girls' bonnets (1887) and a simple pattern for an 18-19in (45.7-48.3cm) doll adapted from a child's doll pattern first issued in 1887. It includes a GUIMPE, SUSPENDERED SKIRT, a darling little HAT of the "Scottish" type and a CAPE.

You will surely also enjoy the little sunbonnet pattern on page 14 with the many possible variations shown on this page of adorable bonnets worn in the 1890s.

So join in the fun and create a costume for your favorite doll or review your knowledge of cartridge pleating, pick up a few tricks for handling of ribbon as trim or just browse through the article on page 15 to learn a few interesting facts about the evolution of patterns to their present-day perfection.

GIRL DOLLS' SET

Material for dress as in front view: 1/2 yd (45.7cm) of plaid material 36in (91.4cm) wide, with 1/4in (22.9cm) of plain material 36in (91.4cm) wide for guimpe.

This charming little dress and hat are illustrated on the envelope of an old doll pattern from 1887. They have been adapted for this book in size 18-19in (45.7-48.3cm) which you may find on pages 5 through 10. The pattern includes a cape with a hood as shown in original pattern and for variations, collars in two sizes.

GIRL DOLLS' SET (consisting of a hooded golf cape, to which we have added a narrow collar and a wide collar for variation, Scotch bonnet, and a dress having a tucked blouse and a separate skirt with or without suspenders).

No.9020:

STANDARD FASHION COMPANY,
NEW YORK, CHICAGO, BOSTON, SAN FRANCISCO, TORONTO.
PATENTED OCTOBER 4, 1887, AND SEPTEMBER 5, 1899.

1899
Girls' and Children's
Anniversary Dresses.
Front
view.
Back
view.
2560
2539
2632
2517
2673
2625
2453
2558
2657
2508
2626
2515

FACTS and FIGURES

1809. LACE. Lace machine patented by John Heathcote (England) for making net on which embroidery was done by hand. Forced out of England by lace craftsmen in 1811, he moved to France and established the French lace industry which flourished.

1813. LACE. Invention of the LEAVERS LACE MACHINE which revolutionized the industry. This machine, modified, of course, is still the basis for modern lace machines which now are so intricately devised that they may have up to 40,000 moving parts, and may control more than 50,000 threads. These machines produce Alencon, Chantilly, Point Venise and Valenciennes or "Val" lace.

1815. LACE. Machine production of lace brought a supply within reach of ladies and gentlemen of moderate means.

1830s. FABRICS. Joseph Jacquard was responsible for a mechanical loom for weaving patterned fabrics.

1850s. READY-TO-WEAR CLOTHING. Dress "kits" were available; a skirt all trimmed and hemmed was sold with a strip of fabric for a band to be attached by the buyer. A matching length of fabric was available for bodice and sleeves.

1850s. SEWING MACHINES. They were first introduced for home use and by 1860, 13,000 had been sold. From this point sales skyrocketed, as more than 20 companies were involved in the manufacture of sewing machines, and some time during the 1860s Singer devised a "time-payment" plan which enabled poor people to make such a purchase where otherwise they would not have been able to do so.

1867. HAND NEEDLES. Hand needles were improved by tapering them at both ends instead of only at the point, thus making it easier to push the needle through heavy fabrics.

1890s. FASTENERS. Snap fasteners appeared about 1897, advertised first as ball-and-socket fasteners, and later as invisible fasteners. (See advertisement, page 16.) Hooks and eyes go back at least to the 15th century in one form or another.

1896, READY-TO-WEAR CLOTHING. By this date ready-to-wear clothing for all ages was being advertised in *Delineator* magazines. A man's suit was priced at $10.00, a lady's suit for as little as $7.50. A small boy's bloomer suit sold for $3.00.

HINTS FOR BIAS TRIM

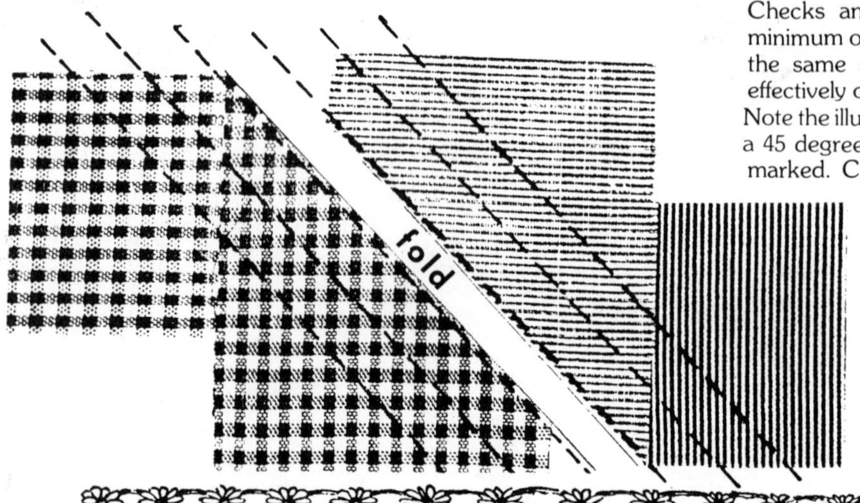

Checks and plaids make interesting bias trim with a minimum of work. The trim may be used on a garment of the same self-fabric plaid, or plaid trim may be used effectively on plain fabrics.

Note the illustration on the left which shows fabric folded at a 45 degree angle to form a *true* bias, with cutting lines marked. Cut strips 1in (2.5cm) wide, fold carefully and press. Turn raw edges down 1/4in (.65cm) and hand stitch in bands around a skirt, two or three rows about 1/8in (.31cm) apart...or refer to HAT TRIM on page 5 for another method of handling bias.

PATTERN INSTRUCTIONS

This pattern was designed for an 18in (45.7cm) doll but can easily be adapted to a 20in (50.8cm) doll — start the skirt with a 12in (30.5cm) x 38in (96.5cm) rectangle, and adjust length of suspenders to fit doll. Guimpe may fit just as it is.

FOR 18in (45.7cm) DOLL.

SKIRT: Cut a rectangle 10in (25.4cm) x 36in (91.4cm) and a lining of the same size if desired.

SKIRT BAND: Cut a rectangle 1¾in (4.5cm) wide and the length of the doll's waist plus 1in (2.5cm) for overlap.

SUSPENDERS: Cut 2 of the pattern piece and cut 2 linings.

HAT: Cut 1 brim and 1 crown of contrasting fabric, also one lining of each.

HAT TRIM: Cut 1 band of dress fabric ON BIAS 2in (5.1cm) x 12in (30.5cm). Cut 1 knotted tie trim of dress fabric about this shape ▱ measuring 2in (5.1cm) x 7in (17.8cm).

ASSEMBLY:

SKIRT: Baste lining fabric to skirt, wrong sides together. Machine-stitch two rows of gathering stitches at top edge, keeping 1in (2.5cm) free at each end for placket. Stitch centerback seam allowing 3in (7.6cm) for placket; turn placket ends and hand-stitch. Pull gathering threads to fit skirt band; lay long end of band on skirt right sides together. Distribute gathers evenly, machine-stitch. Turn band and hand-sew on wrong side, turning in seam allowance at each end. Attach hook and eye.

SUSPENDERS: Place suspender and lining right sides together; stitch all around except between x..........x. Turn inside out, press seams carefully and slip stitch small opening. Trim as desired. Fit on doll attaching on OUTSIDE of skirt band with buttons and buttonholes, or as desired. Suspenders should be 1in (2.5cm) apart in front, 3/4in (2cm) in back.

HAT: Sew centerback seam of brim. Sew centerback of brim lining. Place right sides together, matching centerback and centerfront. Machine-stitch along head edge. Turn inside out, press and baste top edges together.

Baste crown and crown lining together, wrong sides together. Turn brim inside out and set crown inside, matching centerfront, centerback and notches. Baste, then machine-stitch. Finish this raw seam by zigzagging or overcasting. Turn right sides out and press the seam firmly, holding brim and crown together so that the seam stands out a little.

HAT TRIM: Fold bias strip long edges together and machine-stitch. Turn inside out and press. Slip stitch band to hat 1/8in (.31cm) from head edge, starting at centerback.

KNOTTED TIE: Fold and stitch, turn inside out, tie knot and attach to centerback. Sew feather at F.

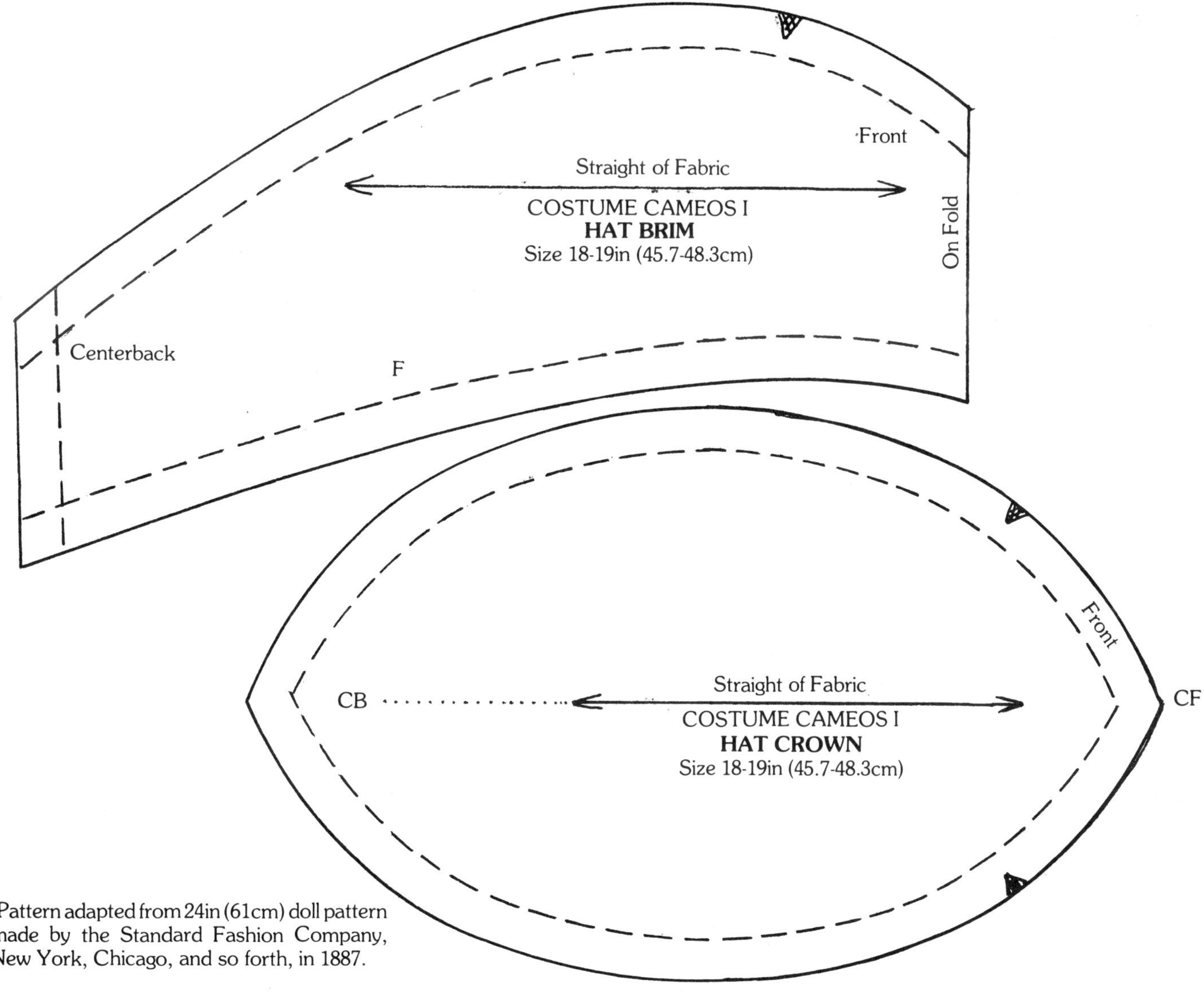

(Pattern adapted from 24in (61cm) doll pattern made by the Standard Fashion Company, New York, Chicago, and so forth, in 1887.

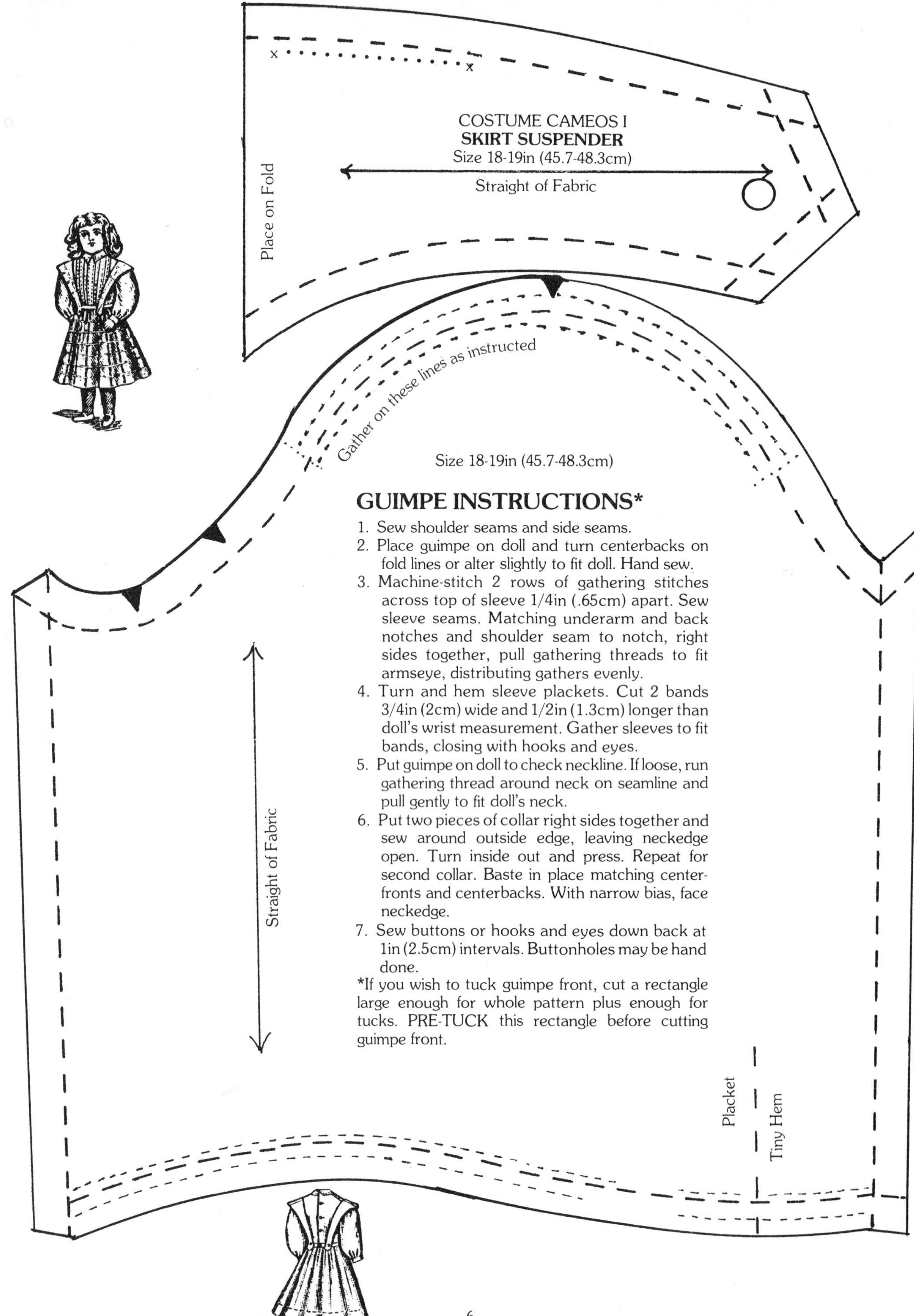

GUIMPE INSTRUCTIONS*

1. Sew shoulder seams and side seams.
2. Place guimpe on doll and turn centerbacks on fold lines or alter slightly to fit doll. Hand sew.
3. Machine-stitch 2 rows of gathering stitches across top of sleeve 1/4in (.65cm) apart. Sew sleeve seams. Matching underarm and back notches and shoulder seam to notch, right sides together, pull gathering threads to fit armseye, distributing gathers evenly.
4. Turn and hem sleeve plackets. Cut 2 bands 3/4in (2cm) wide and 1/2in (1.3cm) longer than doll's wrist measurement. Gather sleeves to fit bands, closing with hooks and eyes.
5. Put guimpe on doll to check neckline. If loose, run gathering thread around neck on seamline and pull gently to fit doll's neck.
6. Put two pieces of collar right sides together and sew around outside edge, leaving neckedge open. Turn inside out and press. Repeat for second collar. Baste in place matching centerfronts and centerbacks. With narrow bias, face neckedge.
7. Sew buttons or hooks and eyes down back at 1in (2.5cm) intervals. Buttonholes may be hand done.

*If you wish to tuck guimpe front, cut a rectangle large enough for whole pattern plus enough for tucks. PRE-TUCK this rectangle before cutting guimpe front.

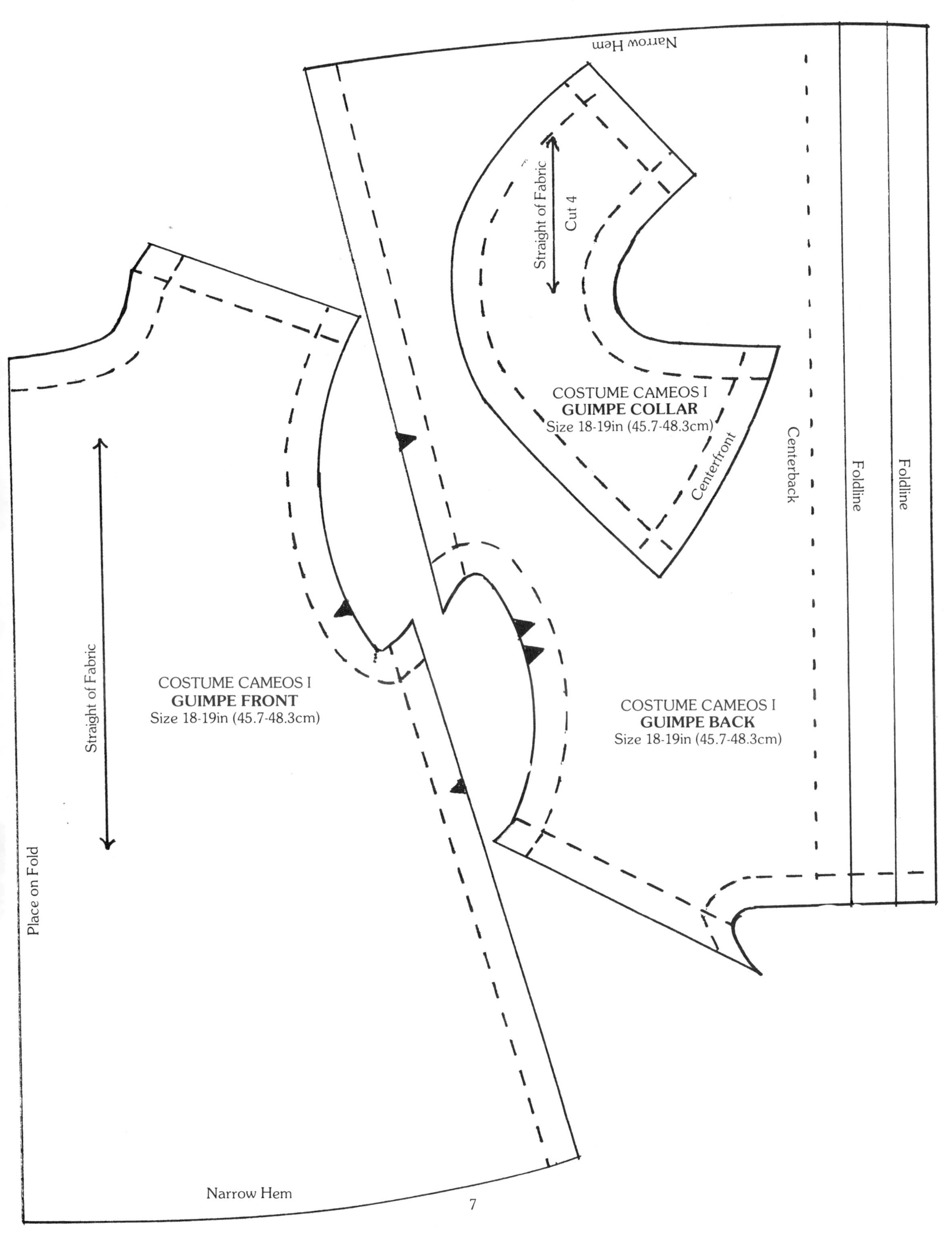
Narrow Hem
Straight of Fabric
Cut 4
COSTUME CAMEOS I
GUIMPE COLLAR
Size 18-19in (45.7-48.3cm)
Centerfront
Centerback
Foldline
Foldline
Straight of Fabric
COSTUME CAMEOS I
GUIMPE FRONT
Size 18-19in (45.7-48.3cm)
COSTUME CAMEOS I
GUIMPE BACK
Size 18-19in (45.7-48.3cm)
Place on Fold
Narrow Hem

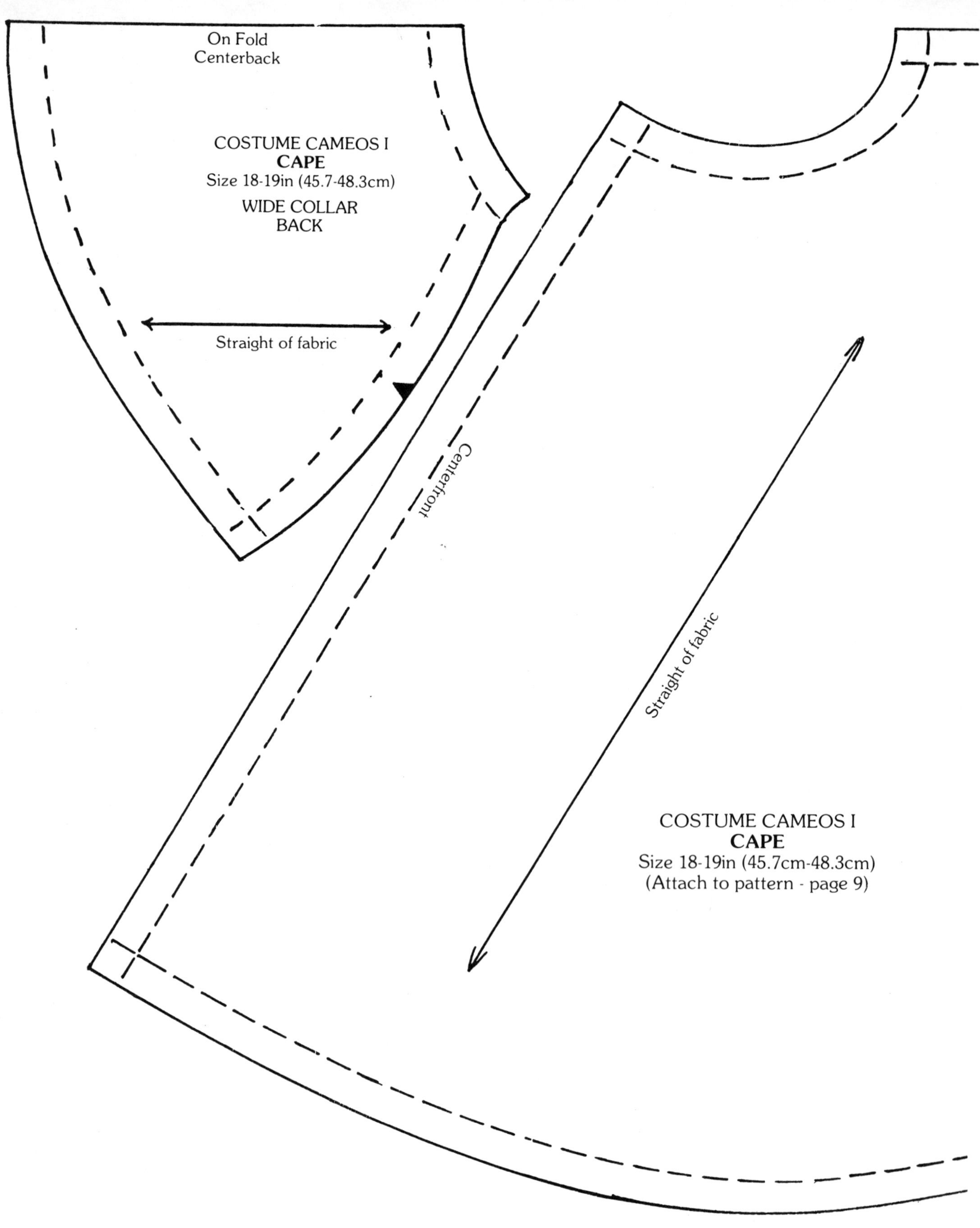
On Fold
Centerback
COSTUME CAMEOS I
CAPE
Size 18-19in (45.7-48.3cm)
WIDE COLLAR
BACK
Straight of fabric
Centerfront
Straight of fabric
COSTUME CAMEOS I
CAPE
Size 18-19in (45.7cm-48.3cm)
(Attach to pattern - page 9)

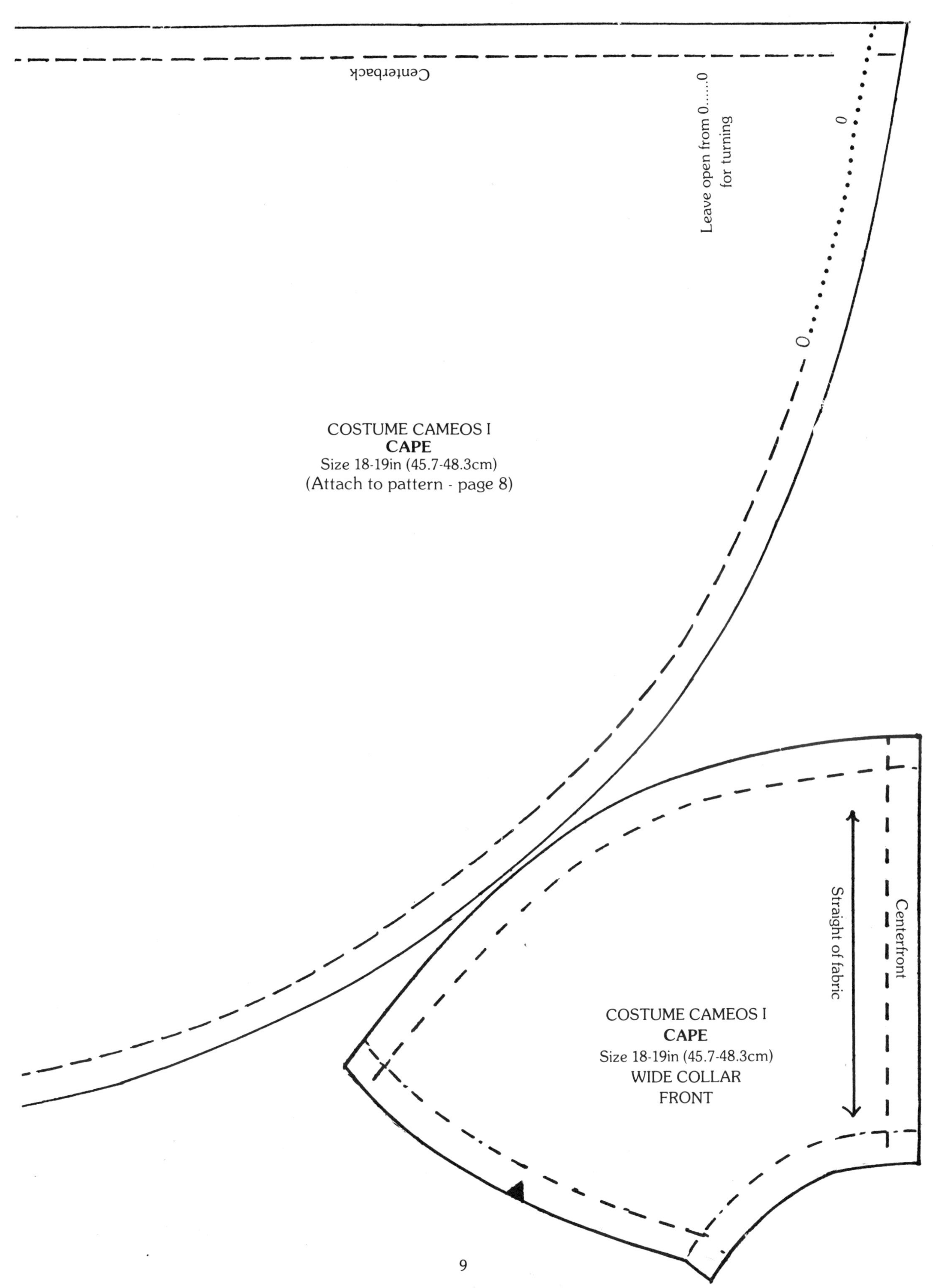
Centerback
Leave open from 0......0
for turning
0
0
COSTUME CAMEOS I
CAPE
Size 18-19in (45.7-48.3cm)
(Attach to pattern - page 8)
Centerfront
Straight of fabric
COSTUME CAMEOS I
CAPE
Size 18-19in (45.7-48.3cm)
WIDE COLLAR
FRONT

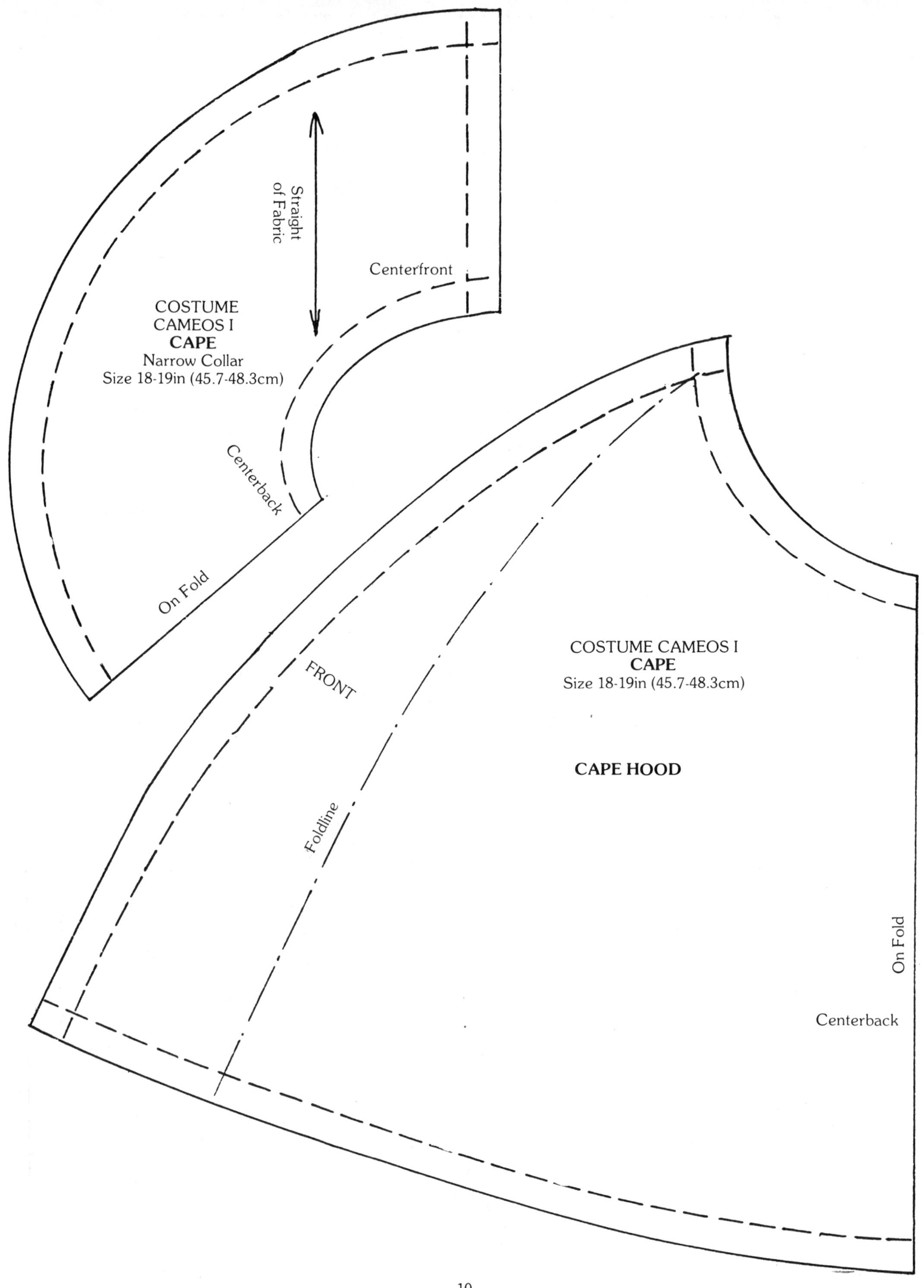
Straight of Fabric
Centerfront
COSTUME
CAMEOS I
CAPE
Narrow Collar
Size 18-19in (45.7-48.3cm)
Centerback
On Fold
COSTUME CAMEOS I
CAPE
Size 18-19in (45.7-48.3cm)
FRONT
CAPE HOOD
Foldline
On Fold
Centerback

CAPE, for Size 18-19in (45.7-48.3cm) Doll

The lined cape shown in our pattern has a lovely hood which falls in graceful folds at the back when not in use, forming a collar effect.

Our own variation of this pattern, adapted from a doll cape of 1900, adds two lovely collars in addition to the hood, one collar rather narrow, the other wider, and falling over the shoulders. The wider collar could be lengthened somewhat as desired and used as a capelette.

CUTTING INSTRUCTIONS

CAPE, View A, with HOOD.

C1. Using a suitable sheer silk or cotton cut 2 CAPE LINING pieces as pattern shows or cut on fold and cut 1 HOOD.

CAPE FABRIC. Cut 2 CAPE pieces and 1 HOOD piece.

CAPE, View B, with collars.

C2. LINING. Using fabric described above, cut 2 CAPE LININGS, and cut 2 COLLAR LININGS, (note that wide collar is in 3 pieces) or if preferred use cape fabric as lining for collars.

CAPE FABRIC. Cut 2 CAPE pieces and 1 complete COLLAR, or cut collar linings of cape fabric.

ASSEMBLY INSTRUCTIONS

Use instructions for both Views A and B, substituting hood for collar as case may be.

VIEW A. CAPE HOOD.

C3. Fold HOOD piece, right sides together, and sew centerback seams. Press open. Repeat for hood lining.

VIEW B. LARGE COLLAR. Place shoulder seams right sides together, stitch and press open. Repeat for lining.

BODY OF CAPE.

C4. Sew centerback seam and press open. Place neck edge of CAPE HOOD around neck edge of CAPE, matching centerbacks. Pin and machine-stitch, clip to machine-stitching at ½in (1.3cm) intervals, and press seams open. Repeat for CAPE HOOD LINING and CAPE LINING, (or for collars) again pressing and clipping.

C5. Place CAPE and LINING right sides together, and machine-stitch all around except from 0..........0. Turn right sides out and press carefully on seamline. Blind stitch open edges together.

TIES

C6. Using 6 strands of polyester thread, or 4 strands of embroidery floss 72in (182.8cm) long, crochet a tight chain. Press. Center chained cord around entire neckline (under collar or at back) and tack all around, and use to tie cape fronts together.

TASSELS for ends of cord. (See illustration.)

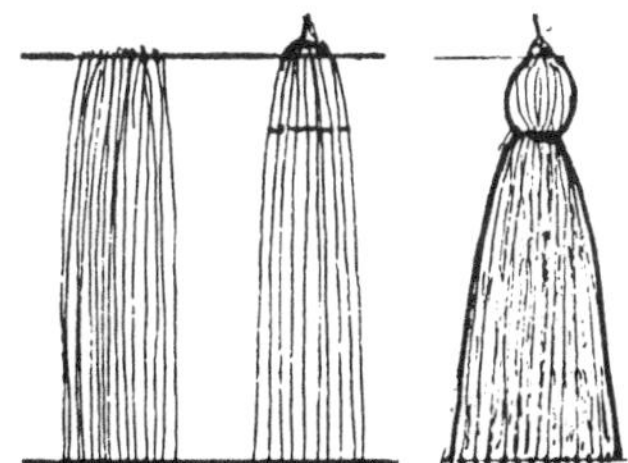

Three steps in making tassels.

C7. Cut cardboard 1in (2.5cm) wide and wind with sewing thread 75 times (or use your own judgment for embroidery floss). Fasten at top as shown, and wind thread around tassel 1/4in (.65cm) from top, and sew tightly in place. Cut bottom edge open. Attach tassels to cord ends.

A tassel may be similarly made and attached to the point of the hood, using any proportions that appeal to you.

COLLAR TRIM.

C8. For WIDE COLLAR, turn at front lower edges as shown in picture and hold in place with tiny buttons.

Braid may also be used around either collar as an attractive trim.

FOR HOOD. Turn back hood without pressing on line shown, to form an attractive frame for doll's face. Also, contrast color of lining will show.

AND THUS IS YOUR DOLL PREPARED FOR WINTRY WEATHER!

Illustration 1. 18in (45.7cm) McKinney reproduction doll with cape, costumed by Hazel Ulseth. *Photograph by Marty Ulseth.*

CARTRIDGE PLEATING

Cartridge pleating is a method of pleating a great width of material to be gathered into a small space, as for example when dressing a china doll with a tiny waist, when you want a bouffant skirt.

METHOD:

1. Cut a rectangle of fabric correct in length for the doll to be dressed, adding allowance for a 1/2in (1.3cm) turn at waist and whatever hem is desired. Turn top edge in 1/2in (1.3cm) and press.
2. With wrong side facing you, start close to the fold, using double thread long enough to cover the full length of the fabric. Stitch in small basting stitches evenly spaced and about 1/4in (.65cm) apart across the length of the fold. (Later you will want to regulate the size of the stitch depending on the weight of the fabric, amount to be gathered and so forth.
3. Place another row of stitches directly below the first row, matching the stitches exactly. (See *Illustration 1.*) In each case do not tie off the thread, but leave ends dangling.
4. Pull threads for both rows evenly to the length desired. You will note that you have the fabric neatly pleated as in *Illustrations 2.*
5. Attach to the bodice or band by catching ONLY the corners of the pleats of the RIGHT side of the skirt and sewing to the band with tiny stitches. The inside bulk will add a little fullness to the outside.

NOTE: Even distribution of pleats can be achieved by dividing both band and pleated fabric into quarter sections and matching these marks.

Illustration #1.

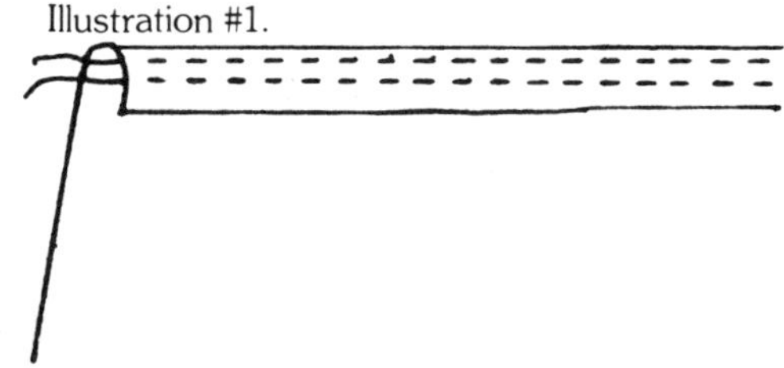

Illustration #2.

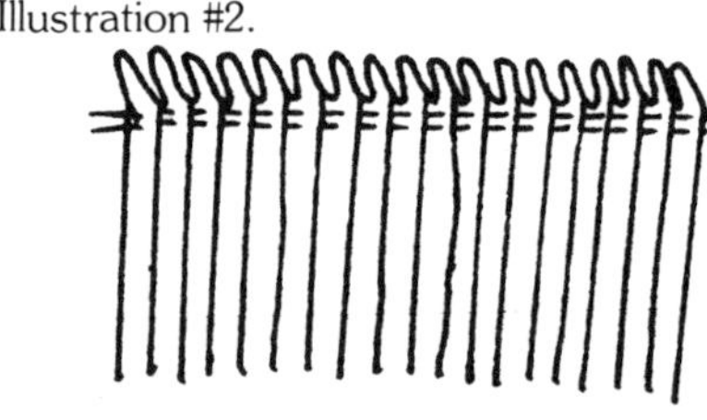

EXAMPLE: For 16-17in (40.6c-43.2cm) doll.

1. Cut a piece of material 13in (33cm) x 38in (96.5cm) on straight of fabric, this allowing for the 1/2in (1.3cm) turn at the top and a 2in (5.1cm) hem. Turn and press 1/2in (1.3cm) at the top.
2. Cut a piece of fabric for band 1¼in (3.2cm) wide and 1in (2.5cm) longer than the waistline of the doll. Fold ends ½in (1.3cm) for placket. Sew as directed for pleating.

EXAMPLE: For 22in (55.9cm) doll.

1. Cut a piece of material 18in (45.7cm) x 48in (121.9cm) on straight ot fabric, this measurement allowing for ½in (1.3cm) turn at the top and a 2in (5.1cm) hem. Turn and press ½in (1.3cm) at top.
2. Cut a piece of fabric for band 1¼in (3.2cm) wide and 1in (2.5cm) longer than the waistline of the doll. Fold ends ½in (1.3cm) for placket. Sew as directed for pleating.

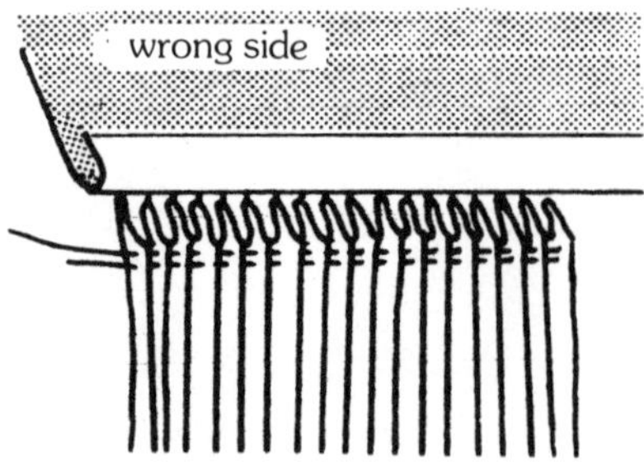

RIBBON

RIBBON HAS MANY USES FOR TRIM OTHER THAN BONNET BOWS AND SASHES. HERE ARE SOME WAYS TO USE IT FOR TRIM THAT ADD COLOR, CHANGE OF TEXTURE AND INTEREST.

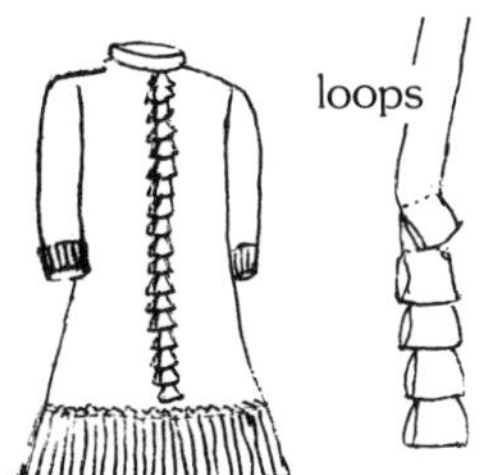

1. Dress front trim. Arrange narrow ribbon in loops, starting from the hemline and working upward, in 1-2in (2.5-5.1cm) loops.

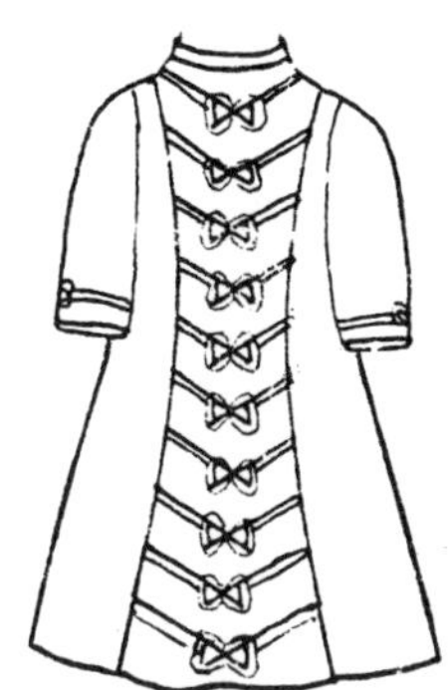

2. Arrange narrow ribbon diagonally in rows down the front of an A-line dress over a contrasting panel. Bows can be added separately after banding is sewn on.

3. Add ribbon trim as shown. Bright ribbon may be used in this way with an overlay of insertions. Again, bows may be added separately.

Ribbon shirred with any of the following patterns of stitching will produce delightfully different designs to be used on the skirts of fashion dolls, bodices or for any other spots where braid trim might be suitable. Using ribbon about ¼-½in (.65-1.3cm) wide, sew in any one of the following patterns:

Stitch on both edges, pull stitches to shirr ribbon and apply to dress.

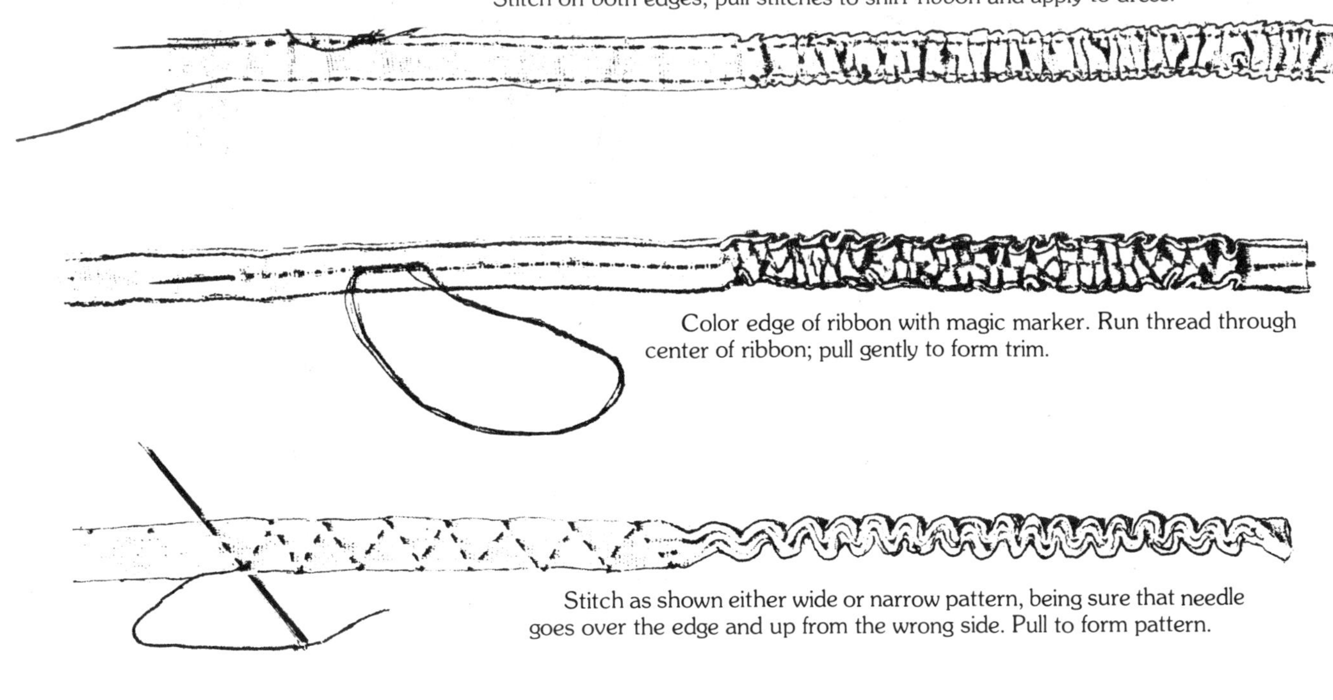

Color edge of ribbon with magic marker. Run thread through center of ribbon; pull gently to form trim.

Stitch as shown either wide or narrow pattern, being sure that needle goes over the edge and up from the wrong side. Pull to form pattern.

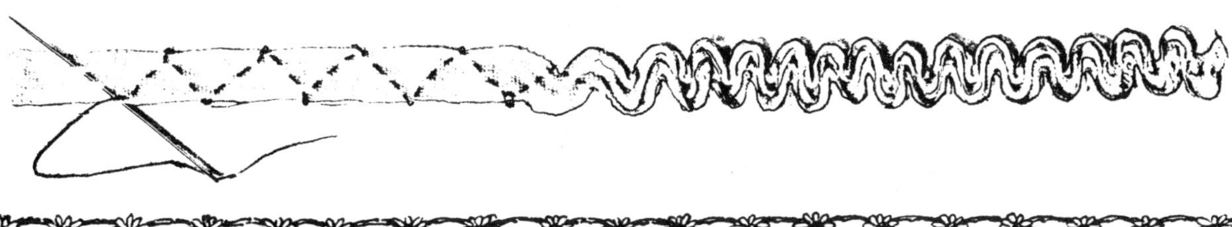

SUNBONNETS 1898

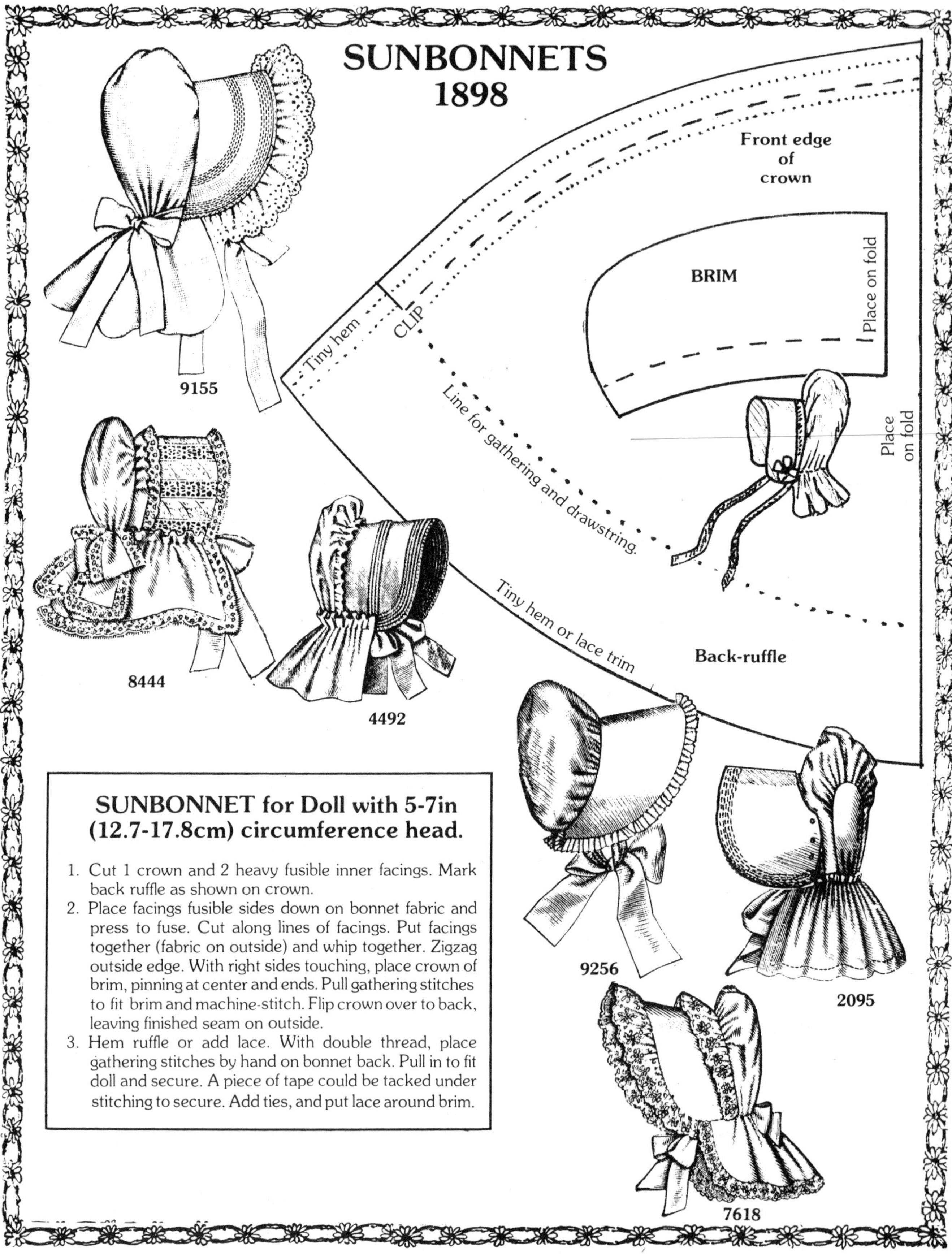

SUNBONNET for Doll with 5-7in (12.7-17.8cm) circumference head.

1. Cut 1 crown and 2 heavy fusible inner facings. Mark back ruffle as shown on crown.
2. Place facings fusible sides down on bonnet fabric and press to fuse. Cut along lines of facings. Put facings together (fabric on outside) and whip together. Zigzag outside edge. With right sides touching, place crown of brim, pinning at center and ends. Pull gathering stitches to fit brim and machine-stitch. Flip crown over to back, leaving finished seam on outside.
3. Hem ruffle or add lace. With double thread, place gathering stitches by hand on bonnet back. Pull in to fit doll and secure. A piece of tape could be tacked under stitching to secure. Add ties, and put lace around brim.

ABOUT DELINEATORS and PATTERNS

Most of us take our fine patterns with all of their intricate instructions and perfect sizing for granted. But can you imagine being without them?

Because of our interest in patterns and their development, we have amassed a few facts about the early fashion books and thought you might enjoy them also.

According to a *Metropolitan Monthly* of February 1874, the Butterick Company started printing patterns in 1865, issuing a *Metropolitan Monthly* as a means of illustrating and advertising their patterns. In 1872 they started publishing their *Delineator* to provide more scope in a larger publication for their patterns, with many more pictures in all categories and sizes including patterns for dolls. The *Delineator* achieved immediate popularity at a cost of 15¢ per issue or a year's subscription offered at $1.50 that included a choice of bonus patterns to a value of $1.00. Prices of individual patterns ranged from 20¢ to 40¢ with a deluxe version sometimes reaching $1.50.

How popular is "popular?" By 1883 circulation was 155,000 copies per month, and ten years later in 1893 it had reached the staggering number of 500,000. Circulation was worldwide, including 85 countries in such exotic and out-of-the-way places as Ceylon, Chile, Hongkong, Congo, Curacao, Fiji Islands, Siam, Sierra Leone, Tasmania, Zanzibar and Orange Free State. Of course, the United States and Canada no doubt subscribed to a large percentage of the total output, but can we just imagine a lady of fashion strolling about in the bush country of Africa wearing her, oh, so fashionable full-skirted, many petticoated costume? It was, in fact, an established practice of the British (the ubiquitous British who were indeed everywhere in their colonial world during this period) to dress for dinner every night even when dining alone, alone in the jungle!

Subscription prices were reasonable enough, at $1.00 per year in the United States and Canada, and $1.60 yearly elsewhere. We do not know what inflation was doing or not doing to the economy in those days, but in 1905 Butterick points out that their *Delineator* magazine was still selling at 15¢ per copy, a price unchanged from 1872.

According to accounts of this era Butterick achieved phenomenal success with their patterns because of appropriate sizing which more nearly conformed to the female form than that of other pattern-makers of the time. Butterick, it was said, had developed a "secret" system of establishing proportions, departing from the practice of other companies who had the idea that these things (sizing for patterns) must be done according to "correct" laws of proportions as found in antique status...Venus de Milo? One can imagine a very correct Mr. Butterick going home with an appeal to his wife to measure herself, the upstairs maid and the plump cook, all of whom in turn probably checked on their friends to find out what ladies actually measured under their voluminous dresses. Whatever the system, they were apparently very successful. According to the same article, Butterick was producing about 15,000 patterns per day, and sending them out to all of the places mentioned earlier.

By 1897 Butterick was not only showing patterns in their *Delineator* magazines, but offered a wide variety of booklets on every conceivable subject of interest to women from sewing to child-care, housekeeping and homemaking, crafts, deportment and so forth.

They introduced the *Deltor* in 1929, an involved and explicit set of instructions for sewing, fitting, cutting and so forth. For many of you reading this article you will remember the days of the more modern *Delineator* patterns, which were finally discontinued in 1937, although Butterick patterns are still with us.

Illustration 2. 18in (45.7cm) Italian reproduction doll with cape, costumed by Hazel Ulseth. *Photograph by Marty Ulseth.*

A PERFECTLY EASY BOW

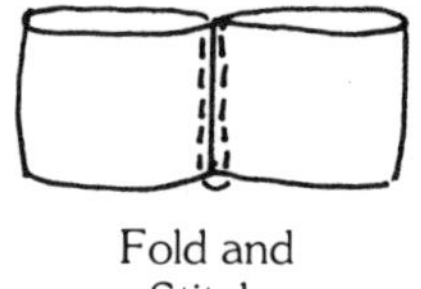

Fold and Stitch

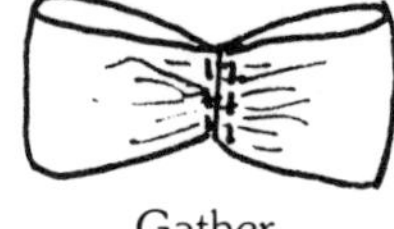

Gather

Add tab

Fold off-center

Combine, tacking at an angle

GLIMPSES of the PAST

ADS from 1880s